I Like to Read

The Picnic

Tina and Bobby were happy.
Their teacher was going to
take them to a picnic.

"Good morning, Teacher,"
said Tina and Bobby.
"Good morning," she said.

"Tina, will you please get all
the children in line?" said
the teacher.
"Yes, Teacher," said Tina.

The children got into line. "Bobby and Sam, Tina and Tanya, are you here?" said the teacher.

"Yes, we are all here," said the children.

"Let's go," said the teacher.
So they all got into the bus.
They all sat down and the
bus started. Soon they
were at the picnic park.

"Here we are at the park.
Take your bags, children,"
said the teacher.
They all got down from the
bus and went to the park.

There were many other
children playing in the park.
"Look at this, Tanya," said
Sam. "Here's a duck."
They looked at the duck.

"Let's play ball," said Bobby.
"Yes, let's play," said Tina.

"Here, catch!" said Bobby.

Tina could not catch the ball.

The ball fell into the water. "Teacher, please help us take out the ball," said Tina. The teacher used a stick to take out the ball.

"Here we are," she said.
"Catch, Bobby."
Bobby caught the ball.
"Thank you, Teacher,"
he said. "Let's play again."

Soon they got tired.
"Let's have something to
eat now," said the teacher.
"Please have some cake,
Teacher," said Sam.

"Tina, will you too have some cake?" said Sam. "Yes, thank you, Sam," said Tina. "I'll have some too. It looks good."

Tina had a glass of milk.
"Mother says that milk is
good for us," said Tina.
"And she says that we
should brush our teeth after
we eat," said Bobby.

"Yes, we will brush our teeth after we go home," said Tina.

After eating, the teacher took out a story book. "Bobby, will you read us a story now?" she said. "Read us this story."

"Yes, I will, Teacher," said Bobby. He read out the story to Sam, Tanya, Tina and their teacher.

Tanya liked the story.
"This is a good story,
Bobby. I liked the story,"
she said.

"I liked it too," said Tina. "And I also liked the picnic. Thank you, Teacher, for the picnic," she said.

"I'm happy you liked the picnic," said the teacher. "Tomorrow, will you write some lines on the picnic?" she said.

"Yes, we will," said Bobby and Tanya, Tina and Sam. "We will write some lines in school tomorrow."

The children played for some time. Then it was time to go back.

"It's time to go back now, children," said the teacher.

"Please make a line. Hurry,
we must get into the bus."
The children stopped playing
and made a line. Then they
got into the bus.

Tanya fell asleep in the bus.
"Wake up, Tanya," said Sam.
"Look, Tina, there's Mother,"
said Bobby.

"Did you have a good time at the picnic, children?" said the teacher.
"Yes, we did, Teacher," said the children.

"May we go home now,
Teacher?" said Tina.
"Yes, you may," said the
teacher.

"Goodbye,
Teacher,"
said Tanya
and Sam.

"Goodbye,
Teacher,"
said Tina
and Bobby.

"Goodbye,
children,"
said the
teacher.

1. Place these pictures in the correct order.